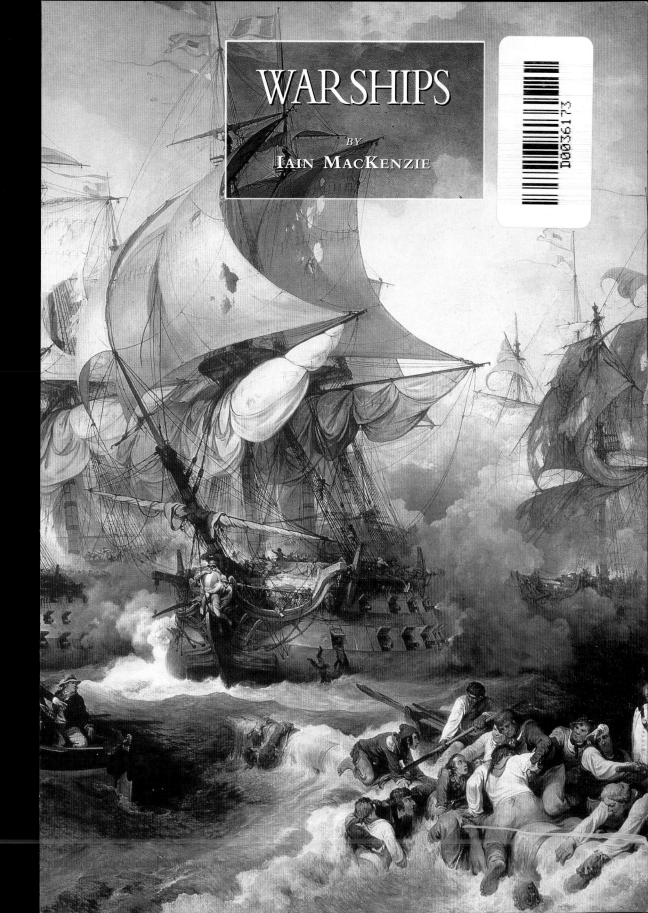

WARSHIPS

BY

IAIN MACKENZIE

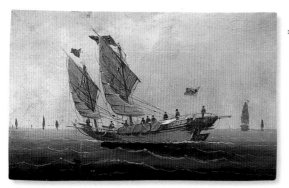

CANTONESE WAR JUNK

Before contact with European navies, warships of the Far East were similar to the trading and fishing vessels of their region. Often the only difference was the war junk's heavy armament and large crew of fighting men. While dangerous, these ships were no match for their technologically advanced Western counterparts.

What is a Warship?

'*He* who commands the sea has command of everything'
Themistocles in 500BC.

From the Minoans of Ancient Crete to the global superpowers of today, seafaring nations of the world have designed or adapted ships for war. An essential means of defence, warships guard one's shores from enemy attack and protect the prosperity which sea trade brings. They can also launch invasions by sea and capture or destroy enemy warships and trade. Because they represent the cutting edge of design, navies have always been an expensive investment: it takes money, skills and costly materials to build and maintain warships, and specialised fighting seamen to operate them. As a result, warships have always been a status symbol - reflecting a nation's prestige and political power. Their development, from paddle-propelled canoe to nuclear-powered submarine, is one of the great stories of human achievement.

DEADLY DESTROYER

Modern warships easily outpower their predecessors. Their hi-tech sensors can detect a threat from many miles away, modern missiles and automatic guns are devastatingly powerful, and satellite communications can send intelligence in an instant. This American destroyer is the first in her class. Weighing in at over 8,000 tons, she is four times the size of a World War II destroyer.

HMS *HOOD*

In the 1920s and 1930s, 'the Mighty *Hood*' was the pride of the British Navy and the biggest warship in the world. Built during World War I, this battlecruiser blew up under fire from the *Bismarck* in 1941. A shell from the German battleship penetrated her armour and hit a magazine (munitions room). Only three members of her crew survived.

HOLLAND'S *NO.1*

Accounts of underwater craft go back surprisingly far – to the time of Alexander the Great. The submarine as we know it was made possible by the invention of the internal combustion engine. The past century has seen submarines develop from experimental craft like the British Navy's *Submarine Torpedo Boat No.1* (designed by JP Holland) to today's 25,000-ton, record-breaking Russian *Typhoons*.

TAHITIAN WAR CANOE

When Captain Cook arrived in Tahiti in 1774, a 300-strong fleet of beautifully decorated canoes came to escort him ashore. Warships have always had great ceremonial importance as a show of wealth and power. The warships of prehistory would have been a craft rather like this one: large canoes, crewed by strong paddlers and fierce warriors.

BLUE SEA, SILVER SCREEN

From the lavish spectacle of Roman galleys in *Ben Hur* to the claustrophobia of *The Hunt for Red October*, sea combat has inspired movie-makers and audiences alike. *The Cruel Sea* (1952) proved a pioneer in its gritty view of World War II.

RULE *BRITANNIA*

The *Britannia* of 1682, one of Charles II's 'Great Ships', was an early First Rate line-of-battle ship. The largest ships of their day, these impressive warships could carry over 100 guns on three decks and needed a crew of over 800 men. Ships like this were the core of the battlefield for 200 years. The *Victory*, Lord Nelson's flagship at Trafalgar, is the only surviving ship of this type

Ancient Times

Our information about the warships of the Ancient World comes from the frescoes of Minoan Crete, the carvings of Egypt and from the art and chronicles of Classical Greece and Rome. The Minoans had a navy by 1600BC, probably the first in the world. Piracy is as old as human history and the Minoans wanted to protect their trading vessels - and to raid other ships! The ancient galley reached a peak in the Greek trireme. In this formidable vessel, with its three layers of oarsmen, the Greeks withstood the Persians at Salamis in 480BC. Recent scholarship and marine archaeology have improved our understanding of ancient naval technology and warfare, enabling the reconstruction of an Athenian trireme. The Romans are not noted for their seamanship, but they defeated Carthage at sea and made the Mediterranean theirs. Rome only contested it again in civil war. The oar-driven galley remained a feature of the 'middle sea' for over 3,000 years.

THE FIRST SEA BATTLE?

This temple relief marks Pharaoh Ramses III's naval victory over the 'Sea Peoples' in 1176BC. Tactics of the day were to grapple an opponent's rigging and try to capsize him, or to board and fight hand-to-hand. These Bronze Age ships were to lightly built to risk ramming an enemy.

The main weapon of the Greek ships was the heavy bronze ram. Mounted low on the bows, it could punch a hole clean through an enemy's hull.

OLYMPIAS REBORN

1987 saw the birth of the Atheniun trireme, the classic warship of the Ancient Greeks. Reconstructed from evidence, this modern replica is formally a ship of the Hellenic Navy. With 170 oarsmen on three levels, she glides along at up to 9 knots. Unlike most galley oarsmen, the crews of the Ancient Greek city-states were made up of free men.

GREEK BIREME

Sails powered the galleys of the Ancient World on the open sea; the skilled oarsmen saved their strength for the attack - they were much more reliable than the wind when manoeuvring in a tight spot.

BATTLE OF ACTIUM

In 31BC a Roman fleet under Octavian wiped out Cleopatra's navy off the coast of Greece. Realising she was fighting a losing battle, the Egyptian queen and her consort, Mark Antony, slipped away to Alexandria and left the rest of the fleet to its fate. More than 400 ships were involved in the battle, imaginatively reconstructed in this 17th-century painting.

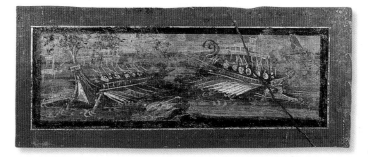

SWORD TO SWORD

Like the Greek warships, Roman galleys had rams, but the Roman soldiers were used to combat on land and preferred to use the spear and the sword. They usually fitted their warships with a hinged boarding plank (the *corvus*) which spiked into an enemy's deck and allowed the soldiers to board the enemy ship and fight hand-to-hand. These small galleys, from a painting excavated at Pompeii, lack the corvus, but the heavily-armed marines are clearly visible.

In time of war, a medieval ruler would demand ships from every port in his kingdom to swell his fleet. The seals and arms of many coastal towns show ships fitted with 'castles', in the bow and stern. These temporary fortified platforms gave some protection to the ship's archers and men-at-arms in battle.

The Dark Ages

Europe's 'Dark Ages', the centuries after the fall of Rome, left little historical record of warship development. However, many Viking warriors were buried on land in their boats and archaeological discoveries have provided much information about the boats of northern Europe and the restless peoples who built them. The 'Norsemen' were experienced sailors. In their longships they explored, raided and colonised. The descendants of these vessels are still used today, for fishing around the continent's northern and western fringe.

VIKING ATTACK!

The collapse of the western Roman Empire around AD 455 threw Europe into turmoil for centuries. The shores of the Baltic, the North Sea and beyond saw several seaborne invasions as restless peoples, such as the Vikings, sought new places to settle. The most fearsome feature of these raiding ships was the fighting prowess and single-minded violence of their crews.

THE VERSATILE VIKING SHIP

Vikings ravaged the coasts and rivers of Northern Europe, from Ireland to Russia. With 'clinker-built' hulls of overlapping planks, these ships were seaworthy enough to cross the Atlantic. The Vikings established colonies in Greenland and North America (which they called 'Vinland'). The longships' shallow draught (how low they sat in the water) allowed them upriver to explore inland.

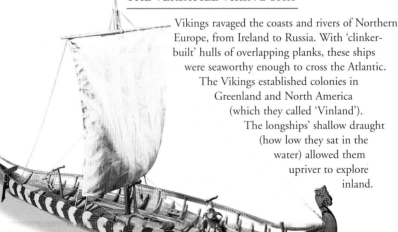

THE TERRIBLE DRAGON

Until recent times, warships
were often highly decorated.
The Vikings favoured a
frightening beast on
the prow, to terrify the
enemy. The dragon
head, or *drakkar*,
gave its name to
the largest type of Norse
warship. The Ancient Greeks
painted an 'warlike glaring eye' above
the ram on their ships, Spanish
galleons were richly painted
and gilded, and 18th-century
ships-of-the-line had carved figureheads
of heraldic figures. Even German submarines
of World War II had insignia on their conning towers.

THE COG

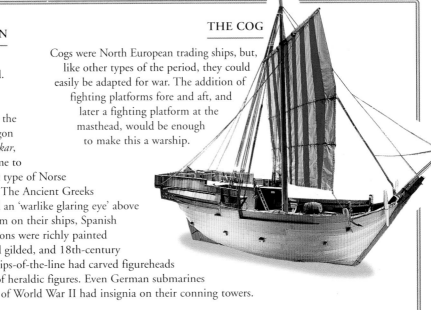

Cogs were North European trading ships, but,
like other types of the period, they could
easily be adapted for war. The addition of
fighting platforms fore and aft, and
later a fighting platform at the
masthead, would be enough
to make this a warship.

PIRATES AHOY!

Large-scale sea battles were relatively rare in the early Middle Ages but
pirates were not! The tactics of fighting at sea were dictated by the
weapons available - the bow, the spear, the broadsword and the battle
axe. Fighting from a greater height gave a crucial advantage and so
the temporary 'castles' soon became a permanent part of the ship's
structure. Another medieval innovation came with
the development of the stern rudder, which
was a great advance on the steering oar.

SEA-GOING FORTRESS

From a 15th-century manuscript,
this imaginary vessel shows a
medieval landsman's notion of an
ideal warship: a wooden castle
garrisoned with armoured men-
at-arms and propelled by oars
rather than sails.

15th~16th Centuries
Carracks to Galleons

*L*ittle is known about the great ships of the 15th and 16th centuries, despite the recovery of Henry VIII's fighting carrack, the *Mary Rose*, which capsized and sank off Portsmouth in 1545. This historic ship's construction suggests she had been rebuilt to carry heavier armament than when she was new, and may have been one of the first generation of ships to fire guns on the broadside. Ships like this resulted from an exchange of ideas and design features over generations of trade between Northern Europe and the Mediterranean. Southern shipbuilding techniques were applied to northern ships, while in the Mediterranean the northern square sail was adopted, creating the 'modern' three-masted ship, which was highly seaworthy and had a large capacity for cargo. The imposing features of the grandest carracks and galleons flattered the vanity of the late Renaissance rulers, and the ships became a byword for wealth and power.

THE GALLEON

The Galleon had finer lines and lower castles than the carrack, making her both faster and easier to handle. Not all galleons were warships, but they were often heavily armed. The type was popular with the Spanish bringing treasures back from the Americas. Long after the true galleon had disappeared, large and richly-laden Spanish ships were known as 'galleons'.

SHIPS OF STATE

This scene shows Henry VIII on his way to meet Francis I, King of France in 1520. The painting was done later and in fact shows the three and four-masted carracks of around 1540. They are equipped with gunports in the hull, though at the time of Henry's visit guns were still mounted on the open decks and in the castles. A huge number of guns were carried by some ships: inventories from the 1490s show some with as many as 200.

'PORTUGUESE CARRACKS OFF A ROCKY COAST'

The *Santa Caterina do Monte Sinai* was a Portuguese carrack of about 1520. She is shown here with the typically vast, billowing mainsail of a Mediterranean carrack. The carrack combined the design and rigging features of the northern cog with the frame-first shipbuilding tradition of the Mediterranean. Three-masted versions were known by the mid-1400s, and in the early 1500s the big carracks were armed with guns that fired through broadside gunports. These were the capital ships of their day.

OAR-SOME POWER

The galley was a common sight around the Mediterranean until the early 1800s. One feature that continued from ancient times was the use of condemned criminals or even slaves as oarsmen. The guns of this Venetian galley are mounted on a platform in the bows - the only place where these lightly-built ships were strong enough to support such heavy weaponry.

FLEETS OF FANCY

A first-rate 100-gun ship was built at Chatham, England in 1670, *Prince* was one of Charles II's 'Great Ships'. Rebuilt and renamed *Royal William* in 1692, she was broken up in 1714. The cost of carved decoration in major warships like this was so high that in 1704 the Admiralty issued orders to limit this fancy 'gingerbread work', as it was called.

THE STERN CABINS

Officers were quartered aft (towards the stern). Each had a private cabin – however small – and the Admiral and Captain had spacious accommodation. But the crew lived in cramped conditions: they had to sling their hammocks above the cannons.

THE POOP

The sails on the mizzen-mast were controlled and signal flags were hoisted from the poop, which was the highest deck.

PUNISHING PUMPS

Wooden ships leak. The bilges, in the bottom of the hull, had to be pumped out regularly. This back-breaking chore was often given to men as punishment for minor offences.

STEERING

The steering wheel was not invented until around 1700. Before then, a vertical pole on the inboard end of the tiller, the whipstaff, controlled the steering.

SHIP'S BONES

The massive oak timbers which made up the skeleton of the ship had to be well-seasoned. Part-completed ships were often left in the shipyard for years to 'season in frame'.

THE SHIP'S GUNS

During the 17th century, the biggest seagoing guns were 'cannons of seven' (42-pounders) and demi-cannons (32-pounders).

SAIL PLANS

The rig of ships evolved during the 1600s. There was much experimentation with sail plans but the versatile three-masted rig was adopted as standard in larger ships. Small craft preferred the single-masted gaff rig, developed in the Netherlands. Here a Dutch warship salutes a Dutch State yacht.

17th-18th Centuries
New Rigs & Types

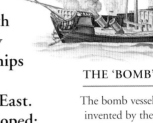

*T*here was little peace in the 17th and early 18th centuries, and when the warring nations briefly ceased their religious and political conflicts, warships were kept busy stopping piracy and protecting the valuable and growing trade with new markets in the East. This was the age when line-of-battle tactics were developed: the 'Great Ships', the first and second-rates with three decks of guns, were built to fight in that line. Smaller ships, forerunners of frigates, scouted for the fleet, and specialist shore bombardment vessels first appeared. It was also the period when artists first began to make reliable portraits of ships in paintings and models.

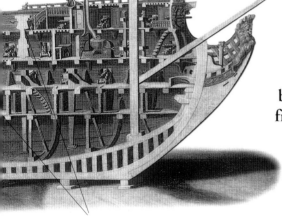

THE 'BOMB'

The bomb vessel, invented by the French in the 1680, carried one or two mortars that fired explosive shells. Built to withstand the shock of firing, this heavy vessel featured a two-masted ketch rig.

ANCHORS AWEIGH!

The only mechanical aids in tasks like raising the anchors or hoisting the sails on their yards were the capstains. They lessened the burden, but still needed strong men to turn them.

PAINTED SHIPS

This model of the English 80-gun third-rate ship *Boyne* of 1692, shows just how highly decorated ships became. Carved by the finest artists and craftsmen, the gilded splendour of the 'gingerbread work' of all classes of warship was typical of the extravagance of the age, and a reminder to the world of the glory of the King.

DUTCH HERO

Michiel Adriaanszoon de Ruyter (1607-1676) was the greatest Dutch naval hero of the 17th century. He was a veteran of campaigns against Spain, France and Sweden and led three wars against England. His most famous exploit was the daring raid on Chatham, England's principal naval base, in 1667. On this occasion his men captured or burnt 16 ships and they took the pride of England's fleet, the *Royal Charles* back to Holland. De Ruyter was mortally wounded nine years later, fighting the French off Sicily.

The Great Age of Sail

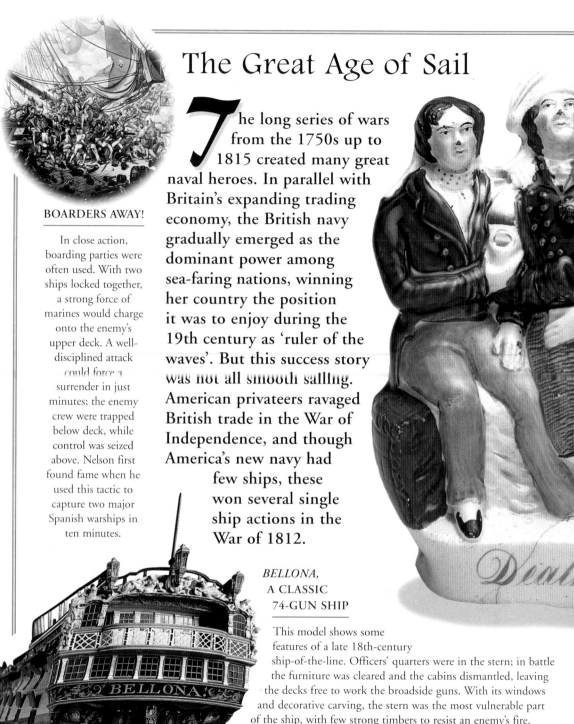

The long series of wars from the 1750s up to 1815 created many great naval heroes. In parallel with Britain's expanding trading economy, the British navy gradually emerged as the dominant power among sea-faring nations, winning her country the position it was to enjoy during the 19th century as 'ruler of the waves'. But this success story was not all smooth sailing. American privateers ravaged British trade in the War of Independence, and though America's new navy had few ships, these won several single ship actions in the War of 1812.

BOARDERS AWAY!

In close action, boarding parties were often used. With two ships locked together, a strong force of marines would charge onto the enemy's upper deck. A well-disciplined attack could force a surrender in just minutes; the enemy crew were trapped below deck, while control was seized above. Nelson first found fame when he used this tactic to capture two major Spanish warships in ten minutes.

BELLONA, A CLASSIC 74-GUN SHIP

This model shows some features of a late 18th-century ship-of-the-line. Officers' quarters were in the stern; in battle the furniture was cleared and the cabins dismantled, leaving the decks free to work the broadside guns. With its windows and decorative carving, the stern was the most vulnerable part of the ship, with few strong timbers to resist an enemy's fire.

The copper cladding on this ship below the waterline was a secret weapon. Copper armoured ships against destructive wood-boring molluscs and algae. Weeds on the hulls of timber ships would grow so long they would create 'drag' and slow down the vessel; copperclad ships remained as fast and streamlined as when they left the dockyard.

'HOT PRESS'

The strict discipline, low pay and long service made going to sea very unpopular. Needing manpower, navies resorted to impressment; the much-feared Press Gangs could forcibly enlist anyone with seafaring experience.

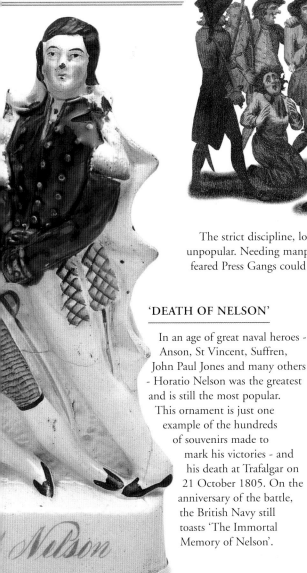

'DEATH OF NELSON'

In an age of great naval heroes - Anson, St Vincent, Suffren, John Paul Jones and many others - Horatio Nelson was the greatest and is still the most popular. This ornament is just one example of the hundreds of souvenirs made to mark his victories - and his death at Trafalgar on 21 October 1805. On the anniversary of the battle, the British Navy still toasts 'The Immortal Memory of Nelson'.

THE LINE OF BATTLE

In the 18th and early 19th centuries, decades of war at sea and constant blockade of enemy ports made the British, in particular, hardened seamen and shiphandlers. A battle line of warships in perfect formation was a thrilling and formidable sight.

THE SMASHING CARRONADE

Introduced in the 1780s, this lightweight gun fired a heavy ball and needed only three or four crew, compared up to fifteen required to operate a 'long' gun. But this gun was only accurate at short range ship armed only with carronades had to run the gauntlet of long range gunfire to close to point blank range. But once at close quarters the heavier carronade ball, and high rate of fire, packed a brutal punch. The effect was so devastating that the gun was nicknamed 'the Smasher'.

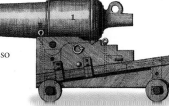

Full Steam Ahead

The navies of the world were slow to adopt steam power for their warships, preferring to wait for the new technology to prove itself. Merchant shipowners, however, were quick to exploit steam, and its independence from wind and tide. The United States was first to build a steam warship, a twin-hulled floating battery for defending New York harbour. Designed by Robert Fulton, the *Demologus* or *Fulton's No.1* was completed in 1815. The British navy began to test steam-paddle warships in the 1830s. But by the 1840s the screw propeller had thoroughly proved itself in a series of tests. The most famous demonstration was made by the screw sloop *Rattler,* when she towed the otherwise identical paddle vessel *Alecto* backwards at 2.7 knots, as both ships steamed full ahead. The arrival of screw propulsion meant that the full potential of steam power could now be put to use, and the first iron-hulled warships were soon in service. Naval warfare was being swept up in the changes brought about by the Industrial Revolution.

BOMBARDMENT

Despite their side paddle-wheels being prone to damage by enemy fire, small steam ships were occasionally used to tow larger sail-powered warships in battle. At the bombardment of Sebastopol during the Crimean War (1854-1856), steam frigates were lashed alongside the battleships, to help manoeuvre the big sailing ships.

HMS *RHADAMANTHUS*

This model shows clearly why paddle wheels were not suitable for warships. Aside from the risk of being disabled by enemy fire, the wheels reduced the space available for mounting broadside cannons. The screw propeller had neither of these disadvantages.

THE *DIANA*

The first steamship to be used in action, and the first to fire rockets in battle, was the East India Company's steamer *Diana*, during British operations against Burmese pirates in 1824. Originally intended just for towing sailing ships, the British Navy fitted her with Congreve rocket tubes. This small ship can claim to be the distant ancestor of today's guided missile cruisers.

RIG OF THE DAY

Uniform clothing for seamen was first issued by the British Navy in the 1850s, over a century after the introduction of officers' uniform in 1748. Seamen traditionally wore loose-fitting trousers, baggy jumpers and short jackets, with a characteristic straw hat and blue collar. The new regulations merely made this style official, as this group at the double wheel of a battleship shows.

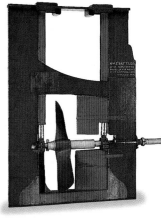

THE SCREW

The screw propeller would not be used for the whole sea voyage. When the wind was favourable ships saved coal by going under sail. The idle propeller had to be moved, to stop it causing drag and delaying the ship. This model was made to demonstrate how the screw could be raised out of the water, into a well in the hull.

A HIDDEN THREAT

Moored mines guarding the approaches to harbours were first used during the Crimean War, which also saw fighting in the Baltic, the White Sea and the Pacific, as well as the Black Sea. The new Russian 'infernal machines' – or 'torpedoes', as they were called – would cause some damage to any ship that triggered one, but the gunpower charge was too small to be really dangerous.

SCREW LINE-OF-BATTLE SHIP

Outwardly little different to a purely sailing warship, this cutaway diagram shows the internal layout of a large steam warship.

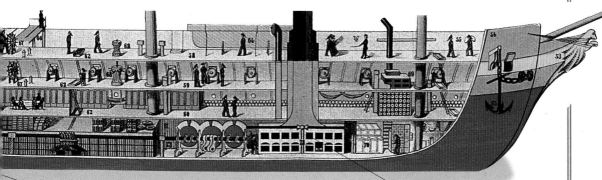

THE LIFTING SCREW

When changing over from steam power to sails, the order *'Down funnel, up screw!'* would be given. It took the whole crew to hoist the heavy bronze propeller.

BULKY BOILERS

Much of the hold had to be given up to boilers, engines and coal, leaving little storage space for provisions.

CLASH OF IRON

The first battle between ironclads ended in stalemate. The fight took place between the Confederate *Virginia* and the Union's *Monitor* in March 1862 during the American Civil War. The *Virginia*, previously the USS *Merrimack*, was a steam frigate converted to an ironclad; *Monitor*, with her revolutionary revolving gun turret, was built to the design of the inventor John Ericsson. Neither ship was entirely seaworthy or effective.

BREECH LOADER

An American naval gun at the Battle of Santiago 1898. Progress in the use of metals and in engineering made breech-loading rifled guns like this the winners in the gun versus armour race. Improved propellant charges, shell design and recoil systems gave the new lighter guns greater accuracy at longer ranges and a higher rate of fire. Nevertheless, navies were slow to adapt to the new technology.

DEVASTATING PIONEER

A step toward the true battleship, the *Devastation* of 1872 was the first truly seagoing warship with no masts or sails, relying on steam power alone. Her iron hull was armoured and she carried her 12-inch muzzle loading guns in centreline turrets, not on the broadside.

FRENCH STYLE

French warship design followed its own path during the last quarter of the 19th century. The barbette ship *Le Furieux* shows the typical 'tumblehome', or inward sloping, of her heavily-armoured sides.

GATLING GUN

In the 1880s, the hand-cranked gatling gun was adopted by several navies and fitted in large warships as a defence against torpedo boat attack: it was also used by naval shore parties in campaigns on land. A century later, close-in weapon systems featuring multi-barrelled automatic guns are again being fitted in warships to defend against the modern equivalent of the torpedo boat, the sea-skimming missile.

From Ironclad to *Dreadnought*

The Battle of Sinope in 1853, in which a Russian squadron utterly destroyed a Turkish fleet of wooden ships with explosive shellfire, was the single event that convinced the world's navies that iron should be the ship-building material of the future. The lesson was reinforced by the damage shells inflicted on French and British ships in shore bombardments during the Crimean War. The French Navy was first to launch an ironclad frigate, the *Gloire*, in 1859. Her structure was traditional oak, but her sides were armoured with 5-inch iron plates. The design revolution was completed a year later, by the British HMS *Warrior*. Built entirely of iron and armoured over a teak backing, she and her sister HMS *Black Prince* outclassed any other ship afloat. With improvements in gun-making techniques and the increasingly powerful performance of steam engines, the naval arms race was on! Naval tactics were updated to take these new technologies into account. Britain maintained the largest navy – outnumbering the combined forces of her two biggest rivals.

JOURNEY'S END

During the Russo-Japanese War (1904-1905), a Russian fleet made a seven-month voyage from the Baltic to Japan. They should have stayed at home! Admiral Togo's skillful fleet overwhelmed them and the war ended in Japanese victory.

ADMIRAL TOGO

Following the opening of Japan to the West in the 1860s, Heihachiro Togo (1847-1934) received his early naval training in Britain. He became commander-in-chief of the Japanese Grand Fleet in 1904. In his flagship *Mikasa* (left), he led his fleet to crushing victories over the Russians at Round Island and Tsu Shima, establishing Japan as a modern naval power.

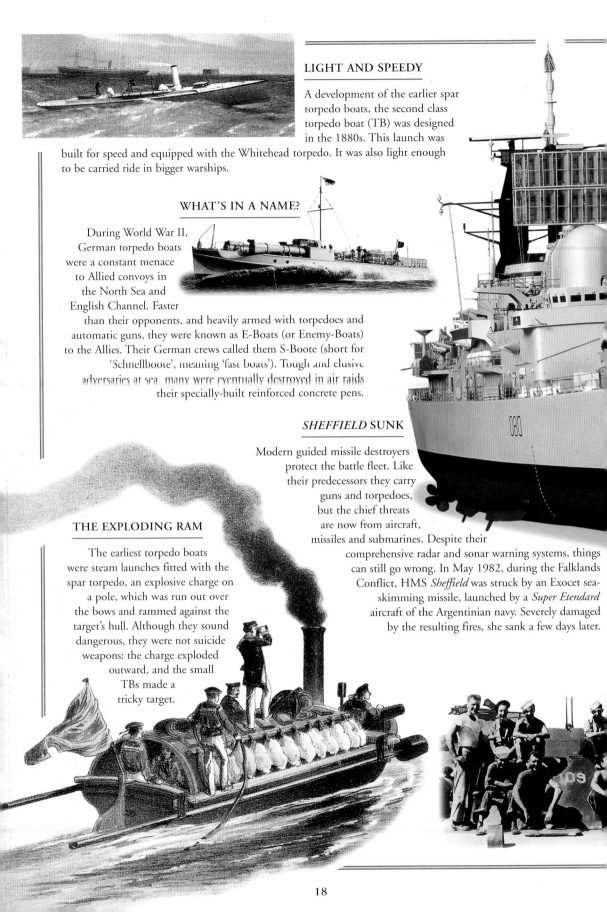

LIGHT AND SPEEDY

A development of the earlier spar torpedo boats, the second class torpedo boat (TB) was designed in the 1880s. This launch was built for speed and equipped with the Whitehead torpedo. It was also light enough to be carried ride in bigger warships.

WHAT'S IN A NAME?

During World War II, German torpedo boats were a constant menace to Allied convoys in the North Sea and English Channel. Faster than their opponents, and heavily armed with torpedoes and automatic guns, they were known as E-Boats (or Enemy-Boats) to the Allies. Their German crews called them S-Boote (short for 'Schnellboote', meaning 'fast boats'). Tough and elusive adversaries at sea, many were eventually destroyed in air raids their specially-built reinforced concrete pens.

SHEFFIELD SUNK

Modern guided missile destroyers protect the battle fleet. Like their predecessors they carry guns and torpedoes, but the chief threats are now from aircraft, missiles and submarines. Despite their comprehensive radar and sonar warning systems, things can still go wrong. In May 1982, during the Falklands Conflict, HMS *Sheffield* was struck by an Exocet sea-skimming missile, launched by a *Super Etendard* aircraft of the Argentinian navy. Severely damaged by the resulting fires, she sank a few days later.

THE EXPLODING RAM

The earliest torpedo boats were steam launches fitted with the spar torpedo, an explosive charge on a pole, which was run out over the bows and rammed against the target's hull. Although they sound dangerous, they were not suicide weapons: the charge exploded outward, and the small TBs made a tricky target.

Torpedo Boats
& Destroyers

The American inventor Robert Fulton first gave the name 'torpedo' (the electric eel) to an underwater explosive charge designed to explode against a ship's hull. When the Austrian Captain Luppus and British engineer Robert Whitehead motorised these devices, it was at last possible to control the depth and course of the charge: the modern self-propelled torpedo was born. Small fast launches, torpedo boats, were quickly armed with the new weapon and soon countered by torpedo-boat destroyers armed with quick-firing guns. At first the destroyers were similar to the small fast boats they hunted. They gradually became bigger and more seaworthy, with a heavier gun and torpedo armament. Destroyers took on an anti-submarine role when the 'sub' replaced the TB as the main threat to the battlefleet. Modern destroyers are large ships, most often with strong anti-aircraft capability. Meanwhile, torpedo boat development has led to missile-armed fast attack craft for coastal defence.

ESCORT

Designed to screen the battle fleet against attack by torpedo boats, destroyers were also used to protect merchant ship convoys in both World Wars. They were not ideal for the task, so new anti-submarine warfare ships such as corvettes and frigates were developed.

KENNEDY'S CRAFT

A typical US motor torpedo boat of World War II, *PT 109* was a fast-striking craft with a killer punch. She was sunk in action by a Japanese destroyer but her commander, Lt. John F. Kennedy (on the right), survived and went on to become United States President.

TIN FISH

The 'locomotive torpedo' was developed by Robert Whitehead from 1860s prototypes, powered by compressed air. Early models could run on a steady underwater course at 6 knots for a few hundred yards: today's computer-guided weapons can reach speeds of over 50 knots.

Submarines

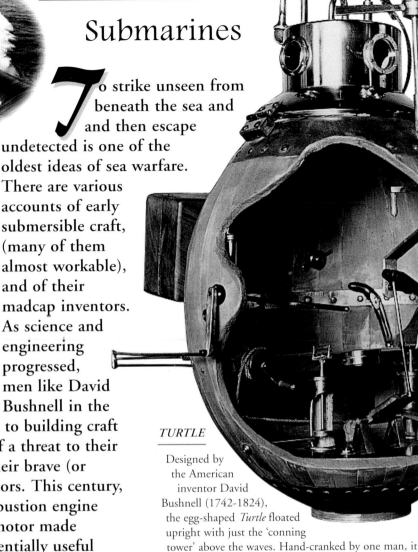

To strike unseen from beneath the sea and and then escape undetected is one of the oldest ideas of sea warfare. There are various accounts of early submersible craft, (many of them almost workable), and of their madcap inventors. As science and engineering progressed, men like David Bushnell in the 1770s came close to building craft that were more of a threat to their targets than to their brave (or foolhardy) operators. This century, the internal combustion engine and the electric motor made submersibles potentially useful ships, with the torpedo filling the last gap. Now equipped with nuclear propulsion, and ballistic missiles with nuclear warheads, the submarine is nearing perfection.

HUNTER-KILLER

The nuclear-powered attack submarine is the major threat to surface ships and other submarines alike. With a range limited only by supplies and crew morale, they can patrol in any corner of the world's oceans. Their streamlined teardrop hulls and silent steam turbines give them a higher speed than any surface warship.

TURTLE

Designed by the American inventor David Bushnell (1742-1824), the egg-shaped *Turtle* floated upright with just the 'conning tower' above the waves. Hand-cranked by one man, it crept along just below the surface, and had a detachable explosive charge which could be fixed to the bottom of an enemy ship. In 1776 an attack on the British flagship at New York was only foiled when the screw that attached the explosive to the enemy hull would not pierce the ship's copper cladding.

ALLIES NOW

Japanese midget submarines tried to mount an attack on Pearl Harbour to coincide with the devastating air raid which opened the Pacific War in 1941, but were detected and sunk. Fifty years later, this *Uzushio* Class diesel-electric attack submarine of Japan's Maritime Self Defence Force is a welcome visitor.

BOOMER COMES UP FOR AIR

The *Resolution* Class of Polaris submarines served NATO's nuclear deterrent force for 30 years. Each sub had two complete crews: one on patrol, the other at the ready. Today the British navy is replacing them with four *Vanguard* Class nuclear-powered ballistic missile submarines, each armed with 16 Trident missiles.

THROWN TO THE WOLVES

In World War II, German U-Boats came close to cutting the essential supply convoys between America and Britain. In bitter Atlantic battles the 750-ton Type VII submarine was a mainstay of the '*Rudeltaktik*' - the 'Wolf Pack' attack.

HOLLAND'S DIVING BOAT

John P. Holland, an Irish emigrant to the United States, was the most successful 19th-century pioneer of the submarine. Thanks to funding from other Irish-Americans, he could develop his prototypes, which he saw as a weapon for use against the British. Following a further cash injection of $200,000 from the US Government, he was able to launch his sixth submarine on St.Patrick's Day 1897. After three years of demonstration and testing, she was purchased by the US Navy and named USS *Holland*. This sequence of photos shows Holland himself, confidently leaving it to the last possible moment to close the hatch as his boat submerges!

DECK GUNS

In addition to their torpedoes, U-Boats were equipped with an 88-mm gun for surface targets and a variety of anti-aircraft cannon and machine guns.

DOUBLE POWER

Running on the surface, powerful diesel engines gave the U-Boats a speed of 17 knots – faster than many convoy escort ships of the day. Submerged, the U-Boat travelled at about 8 knots: the electric motors used underwater were slower but silent.

A TARGET

Defective American torpedoes in 1942 and 1943 meant a lucky escape for many targeted ships, but not this destroyer. By the end of the war, American submarines and carrier-borne aircraft had virtually wiped out both the Imperial Japanese Navy and Japan's merchant fleet.

COLD WAR GIANTS

Each measuring more than 25,000 tons submerged displacement, the six Russian *Typhoon* Class strategic missile submarines built during the 1970s and 1980s are bigger than many World War I battleships.

Cruisers

In the days of sail, 'cruizing ships' were those frigates and smaller line-of-battle ships that were the 'eyes of the fleet'. Steam screw corvettes and frigates developed over the 19th century to go beyond this 'look out' role. They became self-sufficient enough in range, speed and armament to take on a more independent mission: 'showing the flag' or, as a cruiser squadron, patrolling sealanes against pirates. Since World War II the cruiser has returned again to a specialised role. Today's descendants of those original 'cruizing ships' are the guided missile cruisers that provide fleet air defence.

USS *VELLA GULF*

A member of the *Ticonderoga* Class of fleet escorts, the nuclear-powered USS *Vella Gulf* cruiser is equipped with the Aegis air defence system, named after the Greek god Zeus' mythical shield.

HIGH SPEED, HIGH ANGLE

Ships of the *Atlanta* Class of light cruisers fought in most of the US Navy's battles in the Pacific Campaign of World War II. Easily capable of over 30 knots, and armed with sixteen 5inch and up to twenty-four 40mm guns, they were primarily anti-aircraft ships.

FOOD, GLORIOUS FOOD

One of the keys to a crew's morale has always been the food. In sailing days, the ship's cook was usually a former seaman disabled in battle. No knowledge of cookery was required – it was hard to do much damage to salted beef, dried peas and hard tack biscuit! Modern sailors expect and get much better fare.

SHE'S SMOKING!

This Russian protected cruiser built in 1900 served alongside the British fleet in the Mediterranean in World War I. Her five slim funnels earned her the nickname 'the packet of Woodbines', after a brand of cigarettes.

CALL MY BLUFF

The *Deutschland* Class cruiser *Admiral Graf Spee* was scuttled off Uruguay in 1939 after a clever bluff. False information persuaded her captain that an aircraft carrier and couple of battle cruisers were due in Montevideo. It was a trick! He sank his own ship to save his crew and then shot himself. Graf Spee's sister ships *Lützow* and *Admiral Hipper* were sunk in German ports in 1945. Described as 'Panzerschiffe' (armoured ships), the *Deutschland* Class heavy cruisers were only thinly armoured. Still, with their six 11inch. guns in two triple turrets and powerful diesel engines, they had found some success raiding merchant ships during World War II.

NIITAKA

With her three raked funnels, this Japanese cruiser of 1904 is typical of the type in the years before World War I.

SIX-INCH GUNS

This painting shows the sheer scale of a typical World War II cruiser's armament. These guns fired 112-pound shells at a range of 25,000 yards.

BRITISH BULLDOG

HMS *Warspite* was launched in 1913 and served in both World Wars. She earned battle honours in no fewer than 14 major actions including the Battle of Jutland (1916) and the D-Day landings (1944). Her bulldog mascot matches her fighting style – she never gave up.

SMS *HELGOLAND*

The *Helgoland* (right) was typical of German battleships built just before World War I. Like the *Dreadnought* she was an 'all-big-gun' ship, mounting twelve 12inch guns in six twin turrets, and was clothed in up to 12 inches of steel armour plate.

Battleships: WWI, WWII & Beyond

When the British *Dreadnought* was launched in 1906, every other battleship then afloat was outclassed. This revolutionary new capital ship was the first armed with 'all big guns', and had superior firepower and speed to all others. Within 40 years, such battleships would be obsolete because of their vulnerability to modern submarines. Carrier-aircraft assaults, such as the Japanese attack on Pearl Harbour in December 1941, sealed the battleship's doom. Nonetheless, two magnificent examples, America's *Iowa* Class super-dreadnoughts *Wisconsin* and *Missouri*, survived to play a role in the Gulf War of 1991, before being decommissioned to become museums.

HMS *LION*

Heavily-gunned but lightly-armoured, battle cruisers like the *Lion* were relatively fast, but often fatally vulnerable.

Aircraft Carriers

ESCORT CARRIER

A maintenance hangar beneath the flight deck of this World War II convoy escort carrier shelters the aircraft when not on anti-submarine patrol.

Aircraft first flew before the *Dreadnought* was even built. By 1914, 16 seaplanes caused a stir at the British navy's Fleet Review. The first take-off from an anchored battleship had been in 1910, and a seaplane carrier was with the British Grand Fleet at Jutland in 1916. By World War II, aircraft carriers were supreme. They enabled planes to cross the vast Pacific to destroy the American ships at Pearl Harbour, on 7 December 1941. In the Atlantic too, the convoy escort carrier groups eventually cleared the U-Boats from the sea. Today, nuclear-powered aircraft carriers play a vital role in deterring aggressors with their looming offshore presence.

HORNET

Each *Nimitz* Class carrier operates two squadrons of *F/A-18 Hornet* supersonic fighter/attack aircraft. This twin-engined craft requires only one or two crew for its fighter or attack missions.

FLOATING AIRBASE

Over 1,000 feet long, weighing in at over 100,000 tons when fully laden, and with a total crew of 6,000 sailors and airmen, the *Nimitz* Class nuclear powered aircraft carrier USS *Abraham Lincoln* is second to none. The US Navy operates no fewer than six of these giant floating airfields, and has two more under construction. Each carries up to 72 fixed-wing strike and reconnaissance aircraft – a force to be reckoned with.

HIGH-TECH AIDS

In contrast to the bare expanse of the flight deck, the carrier's bridge is crowded with hi-tech equipment used for communications and navigation. It takes a highly-trained, disciplined crew to operate one of these enormous ships.

ABANDONED SHIP

This Japanese aircraft carrier, the *Akagi*, was planned as a battle-cruiser but converted while building. She was set on fire by American dive bombers at the Battle of Midway in 1942, and had to be scuttled.

A TOWN ADRIFT

Modern carriers require crews the size of a small town. And the men and women who live on them have a town's facilities at hand. Here the ship's barber trims a 'flat-top' - other styles available on request!

CORSAIR

First used over Vietnam, the *A-7 Corsair* was in service with the US Navy for 25 years. She is affectionately known as 'SLUF'. Short Little Ugly Fella!

SHIPS' STORES

The modern fleet, often at sea for months at a time, relies on its fleet train of auxiliary ships to provide the backup of stores, fuel and ammunition. Modern supply ships like the British Royal Fleet Auxiliary Service's *Fort Grange* Class provide the front-line ships with everything they need. Able to carry troops and helicopters, they can also support amphibious (on-land) operations. For self-defence they are armed with a few light anti-aircraft guns.

MARINES

Major warships carry a detachment of elite troops trained in all aspects of raiding and commando warfare. They can be put into trouble spots by their ship's helicopter or, as here, by fast rigid inflatable craft. Whichever nation they belong to, these 'sea soldiers' are fiercely proud of the traditions of their corps.

GUIDED MISSILES

This harpoon would not be found in a whaling ship! The Macdonnell Douglas Harpoon missile is radar-guided and accurate to 70 nautical miles. Almost as fast as Concorde, this powerful anti-ship weapon carries a 227kg warhead. The slower Tomahawk SLCM (ship-launched cruise missile) can carry a nuclear or conventional warhead to a land target at a range of 700 nautical miles.

SHIP'S BRAIN

Ships in battle were once controlled from the quarterdeck or the bridge, but the Combat Information Centre (CIC) is the 'brain' of the modern warship. Sophisticated radar and sonar equipment can detect any threat and computer guided weapons and countermeasure devices will deal with it. Pinpoint satellite navigation systems and communications links bring an accuracy that admirals of the past could only dream of. The men and women of modern navies have to keep up with all this technology and are constantly mastering new techniques.

Warships Today

The demands on modern navies are as varied now as at any time in the past. With the Cold War long behind us, the emphasis is on peacekeeping rather than war. Today's warships are used to police international security agreements. The importance of air superiority to many of these tasks ensures that aircraft carriers and carrier groups remain central to naval plans. But new technologies, and the race to stay ahead of the threats that they pose to warships, are already changing the shapes and capabilities of the next generation of cruisers and destroyers. As with every development in ship design over the centuries, these changes are affecting not only tactical and strategic matters, but the way every ship is commanded, and even the demands upon each member of the crew.

ARMS CACHE

Where once cruisers had menacing gun turrets, this US Navy *Ticonderoga* Class cruiser has apparently plain areas of deck. But, hidden beneath the hatches, there are over 120 land-attack, anti-ship and surface-to-air guided missiles at the ready, all precision-controlled by the ship's sophisticated technical systems. Just in case, these cruisers also carry automatic 5inch guns, torpedoes and rapid firing anti-missile defences.

USS *ARLEIGH BURKE*

First of her class of 28 ships, this 1991-built destroyer has the rakish look of those of the past but capabilities none of them could match. Equipped with the Aegis system, she is designed for an air defence role, and armed with missiles, guns and powerful electronic countermeasures. Ten future ships of this class will carry a helicopter, adding to an already impressive range of abilities.

Into the 21st century

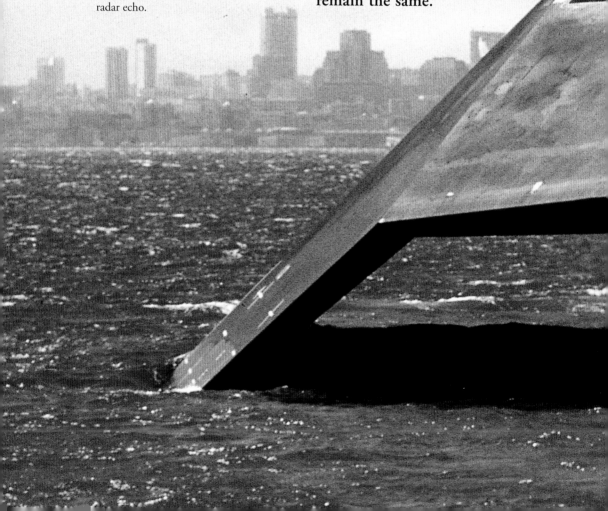

The warships of the future may look very different to the current generation of vessels. 'Stealth' technology will give rise to strange angular shapes, which minimise a ship's radar signature. Hull forms such as catamarans and trimarans may be adopted, new materials will become available, 'smart' weapons will be replaced by 'brilliant' ones and advanced propulsion systems will make ships and submarines quieter and ever harder to detect electronically. But of course, there will be advances in the means of detection at the same time. With new technologies will come new ships and new seamanship. Only the ancient hazards of the sea will remain the same.

PROJECT HORIZON

As warships become ever more expensive to design and build, seafaring nations are pooling their resources. In Project Horizon, the British, French and Italian navies are already producing the next generation of surface warships. Note the uncluttered sloping super-structure; with no hard edges, this ship will give very little radar echo.

THE SHAPE OF THINGS TO COME

A design proposal from the innovative warship builders Thornycroft, the *Sea Wraith* corvette explores the angular sculptural forms of stealth technology. To some eyes, her long, low proportions and the backward raking bow hark back 2,500 years to the Athenian trireme.

ELECTRONIC CAMOUFLAGE

In service since 1996, *La Fayette* has many of the features that will soon become familiar. Angled surfaces disperse the signal from incoming radar, while amazing new materials and paints absorb much of the rest. This frigate will be with the French fleet for many years to come.

FLOATING LABORATORY

The *Sea Shadow* has been in service since the early 1980s. On this floating test-bed, the US Navy experiments with new materials, equipment and techniques. The lessons learnt here will affect the development of warships in the 21st Century.

DID YOU KNOW?

If you cross a Nubian with a Zulu, you get a Zubian! *Tribal* Class destroyer HMS *Nubian*'s bows were torpedoed in October 1916; just ten days later her sister ship, HMS *Zulu*, had her stern blown off by a mine. Both ships reached harbour despite the damage. There, the stern section of the *Nubian* was fitted to the undamaged bows of the *Zulu*. HMS *Zubian* entered service in 1917.

The navies of the world are shrinking. At the end of World War II the US Navy numbered over four million personnel. By January 1997, there were 618,322 officers and enlisted personnel serving in the US Navy, Marines and Coast Guard.

Ships can salute. When a warship and a merchant vessel meet at sea, the merchant ship must salute by dipping (lowering) her ensign, and the warship dips hers in return.

Young boys manned warships. Boys as young as 10 and 11 were part of the crews of warships in the past. While learning their trade as seamen, they also acted as servants to the ship's officers, and in action they carried powder from the magazine to the guns.

Cleopatra was not the only queen to run away from a sea battle. The Greeks won victory over the navy of the Persian King Xerxes at the Battle of Salamis in 480 BC. During the battle Queen Artemisia of Halicarnassus, an ally of the Persians, saw she had backed the losing side. To make her getaway, she rammed and sank one of the Persian galleys. The Greeks, thinking her ship must be one of theirs, did not interfere with her escape!

There are over 150 old warships preserved as museums throughout the world. These include a sailing line-of-battle ship (HMS *Victory*), frigates, ironclads, sail and steam corvettes and gunboats, cruisers, submarines, torpedo boats, aircraft carriers and battleships. Members of the public can go aboard and experience (or imagine) how sailors lived and fought in past wars.

A ton needn't weigh a ton. Warships' tonnage is not the same as merchant ships'. Nowadays warships are measured by their displacement - that is, the weight of water they push aside when afloat. This means the tonnage of a warship is (more or less) the weight of the ship in tonnes. The figures for a merchant ship measure deadweight tons – how much cargo they can hold.

Storms were more successful than ships against the Spanish Armada. In 1588, as the Spanish Armada crossed the English Channel, only a handful of Spanish ships were lost in fighting with the English fleet. More than 10 times as many were wrecked in storms as the Armada sailed home. Through the ages, disease and accidents on board ship have always been a threat: seamen used to say that their doctors killed ten for every one killed by the enemy.

Warships are recycled. When wooden warships were broken up at the end of their useful lives, the precious timber was often salvaged and used for other purposes. Some timbers from the *Bulwark* and *Agamemnon*, 19th-century British-built warships, were used in building a famous London department store!

ACKNOWLEDGEMENTS

Consultant Editor: Pieter van der Merwe, National Maritime Museum. We would like to thank: Graham Rich and Clare Oliver for their assistance. Picture research by Image Select. Printed in Italy. Copyright © 1998 ticktock Publishing Ltd., UK.

First published in the U.K. by ticktock Publishing Ltd., U.K., in association with the National Maritime Museum, Greenwich. All rights reserved. No part of this publication may be reproduced, stored in a retrieval system, or transmitted in any form or by any means, electronic, mechanical, photocopying, recording or otherwise, without prior written permission of the copyright owner.

A CIP Catalogue for this book is available from the British Library. ISBN 1 86007 031 0

Picture Credits: t=top, b=bottom, c=centre, l=left, r=right
AKG; 4tl, 6/7c, 6L, 20/21B. Ancient Art & Architecture; 4bl. Ann Ronan @ Image Select; 16tr, OFC & 17tr, 21tr, 15b. Anton Otto Fisher/Vallejo Gallery (USA); 19tr. British Library; OFC, 7tr & 32c, 11tr. Bridgeman; 5br, 7l, OFC & 7br, 18tl. The Defence Picture Library; OFC , 21br, OFC & 22bl, 29tr, 30tl. et archive; 25tr. Frank Spooner Pictures; 28/29cb, 30/31, 31c. Giraudon; 5bl, OBC & 8tl. Image Select; 17br, 23t. The Kobal Collection; 3br. The Military Picture Library; 22tl, OBC & 26b, 27tr, 27tl, 28b, 28l. National Maritime Museum; IFC/1, 3tl, 2tl, 2/3cb, 2/3c, 5tr, 6tl, 8bl, 8/9c, 9t, 9b, OFC & 10br, 10tl, 10/11c, 10bl, 11br, OBC & 13tr, 13cr, 12bl, 12/13c, 12tl, 13b, 14bl, 14r, 15tr, OFC & 14tl, OBC & 15c, 15tl, 16tl, 16bl, 16/17c, OBC & 18r, OBC & 18bl, OFC & 19br, 22/23c, 23r, OBC & 24tl, 25tl, 26tl. Royal Navy Submarine Museum; 21tl, 3tr, 20tr. US Navy; 20tl, 22br, 27c, OBC & 26/27ct, 29br. US Department of Defense/Corbis; 2bl. US Navy (National Archives); 18br, 18c, 22tr. Vosper Thornycroft (UK) Ltd photographic department; 31tl.

Every effort has been made to trace the copyright holders and we apologise in advance for any unintentional omissions. We would be pleased to insert the appropriate acknowledgement in any subsequent edition of this publication.

snapping-turtle guide